A PRACTICAL GUIDE TO ASCENSION
WITH ARCHANGEL METATRON

A Practical Guide to Ascension
with Archangel Metatron

Kristin Taylor, JD, LLM

A Practical Guide to Ascension with Archangel Metatron
by Kristin Taylor

© 2019 Kristin Taylor.

ISBN-13: 978-1-63227-288-1 Print
ISBN-13: 978-1-63227-289-8 Ebook

www.kristintaylorintuitive.com
For permissions contact:
info@kristintaylorintuitive.com

Cover design by Sheila Brand.
Book layout and design by Sarco Press.

For Archangel Metatron, my friend, mentor and guide. Thank you for asking me to work with you and for opening my mind to how beautiful my life and work could be. Thank you for always being there, for your patience with me and for believing in me, even when I didn't believe in myself. I am eternally grateful.

For Marsha, my Earth angel.
Thank you for everything.

For Jim, thank you for your inspiration.
I finally wrote that book.

Contents

Preface

I'M SO PLEASED that your journey has led you to this book and to invite Archangel Metatron into your life. The magic is just beginning!

I wasn't sure what to expect when Metatron came to me so many years ago. Here was a beautiful, huge light being in my bedroom, flashing light and geometric shapes all around me. His presence is immense. I had been working with archangels for some time but had not experienced anything like this before.

It took a long time for me to know and trust Archangel Metatron. It actually took many years to build the level of relationship that I have with him now, where I can say that I am his devoted student and channel. I had no idea that I would leave my corporate law practice to be a full-time Metatronic channel and teacher. Yet, I am happier than ever, and this increases daily.

To me, Metatron is a trusted friend, ally and companion. He gives me guidance, and I have learned to trust it. I have always been sorry when I haven't followed his guidance, but he has never forced me or violated my free will. He doesn't even offer his guidance unless he is asked, or unless it is a matter of great importance.

Metatron asked me to write this book some time ago, and I got really excited when I learned it was about ascension. I personally feel that a lot of clarity is needed in this area. It's always described as this vague spiritual topic, and I prefer practical and grounded spirituality.

Archangel Metatron's specialty is ascension, or what he calls "personal ascension." In this book, Metatron has thoroughly explained ascension in a very approachable, concise and understandable way. He is here to help each of us to become lighter and freer, to release the past and to embrace a beautiful future.

Metatron is especially focused on those who are willing to hear his call and do the necessary work. These individuals have been called "lightworkers" and the most dedicated of this group are referred to as "wayshowers." Wayshowers, such as myself and my advanced students, light the path for others; however, anyone can choose to work with Metatron.

As I understand it, Metatron asked me to work with him because I came here to be a wayshower and have worked with him in many other lifetimes. I'm also willing to release my past and do whatever is needed to move forward in a brighter and happier way, helping others to do the same.

He also asked me to work with him because I am a former corporate lawyer and have a very logical way of thinking. When I decided to embark on a career in spirituality, I had the goal of helping people in concrete, practical ways. It turns out that Metatron has the same goal, and so we work very well together. Even better, his energy is so powerful that working with him can bring very fast and effective results.

I have always had the vague sense that it was possible to feel lighter and happier, even though I didn't previously know how to do it. I am so pleased to be in communication with a beautiful light being who helps me with practical steps, and I am honored to share these steps with you in this book.

Metatron will ask that you look at everything which needs to be released. I have often had to have great courage to overcome the resistance and fear of doing this. That old secret guilt or shame you don't want to face? That relationship where you felt to blame? Your painful childhood memories? It doesn't matter what it is. If you choose to continue to work with Metatron, you will have to face all of it, and sooner rather than later.

Metatron stresses that we have to release all old energy that is weighing us down. We don't have to do this immediately, but he asks for consistent effort. Of course, he helps us every step of the way. Combine these efforts to release the past with the energetic upgrades that Metatron gives us when asked, and real change can be achieved.

I have unknowingly been on Metatron's plan for ascension ever since I met him in this lifetime, even though I did not channel anything about ascension for many years. Now I lead my students along this path, and I have outlined it, with Metatron's help, in this book.

Following Metatron's plan for personal ascension has made me happier and happier. Problems have fallen away, and my life and body have become more and more aligned. Unhealthy relationships have either become healthier or have not remained in my life. I have felt more part of the oneness than ever before, and I feel a deep sense of love and connection on a daily basis.

Working with him is like working with a beautiful beam of light. The main reason I chose to become a channel of light (besides being guided) is how it feels to be constantly bathed in the blissful divine energy. Metatron always makes me feel better and makes my life more beautiful in so many ways. He improves my relationships, my mood and everything about my life. He is pure magic.

Many people have written books about angels, and you might be wondering how this one is different. The answer is that it is practical. This book outlines the precise steps you need to take to change your life and nothing more. If Archangel Metatron is anything, he is practical and to the point. You will not find fanciful or elaborate new age explanations, but you will find real, solid information that can really bring positive changes if you follow it.

You will need a journal and a pen or pencil to complete the exercises in this book. The audio meditations, which can be found on my website as indicated, are also powerful and highly recommended. It is advisable to work through the book in order, taking the necessary time to complete each section before moving onto the next. Worksheets (journal pages) also can be downloaded from my website. Case studies of some of my advanced channeling students can be found at the end of the book.

You will get as much out of this process as you put into it. If you really dedicate yourself to the exercises in this book, the results can truly be life-changing, just like they have been for me and for many others. Whatever is going on for you in your life, working with Metatron can help to make it easier and better.

If you choose to become a Metatronic channel like me and my advanced students, even more positive transformation awaits you. Again, this is always your choice.

In any case, if you are reading this, you have heard Metatron's call. This is certain. Don't worry if you haven't felt him come to you like he did with me, or haven't seen any flashing lights or geometric shapes. I have heard many other similar reports, but this does not have to happen to be called to work with Metatron.

I am so excited for your journey. Great happiness awaits you!

Kristin Taylor
January 10, 2019
London, UK

CHAPTER 1
Introduction from Archangel Metatron

WE WISH TO invite you to take part in a global awakening which is known as the "ascension" process. You will already be taking part in it on some level without even realizing it. We would like to help you to make this process conscious. It is a much more effective transition if you are aware of it and if you can purposefully assist with it.

The Earth is being called to rise up in energy and in love. The dark days are over and, as a planet, all humans are healing and releasing the past. Humans are also connecting to lighter and lighter energies as frequencies become lighter.

We have spoken before that it is a fallacy that

the ascension process happens at the collective level. The effect is collective but the origin is not. The origin is always at the personal which is the subject of this book. In it, we will illuminate several ways in which to work with us and to hasten the process of ascension for each of you.

What is Ascension?

Each human is composed of varying densities of matter. This is law. What is not seen with your instruments and science is the weight of energy. It can be very dense, and yet it cannot yet be measured by humans.

Many of you, especially those of you identifying yourselves as lightworkers or working in the healing arts, are already aware of how a person feels lighter after releasing a particularly "heavy" and upsetting topic from their past. Even the word used to describe it gives it away - "heavy." Healers further know that past events and patterns can create illness in the body. When the past energy has been released, then often the body can heal from the manifestation of the energy - the heaviness.

We wish for you to think of old energy in this way, as having a physical weight. Light and loving experiences do not weigh anyone down. It is the traumatic or hurtful events which create "heavy" energy and an imbalance in the human body.

In the ascension process, we systematically remove the causes of heavy energy in the body. You will discover in this book that there are many causes and indeed most humans have them all. This is normal.

As the old energy is removed, the human being feels lighter, freer, healthier and overall better. It takes some effort and conscious attention, yet the results (happiness, joy, love, freedom) are more than worth it. In fact, the highest state of being for any human is to reach the ascended, enLIGHTened state. We wrote enLIGHTened like that because it actually is a process of LIGHTENING the energies by removing heavy energies from the energy field of the being.

This is critically important and cannot be overemphasized. It can be said that **your level of happiness, synchronicity, bliss, and feelings of wellbeing are DIRECTLY linked to the heaviness or lightness of your energy field.** We assert whole-heartedly that this is science and yet it is yet to be fully discovered and accurately measured by your scientific systems, which do not adequately account for energy in the context of the human being. This will be changing in the not-so-distant future, certainly within your lifetimes.

Thus, can you see how the ascension process and the LIGHTening of the being are so incredibly important? You could accurately say that there is no work that is more important for each of you to undertake. You also can accurately say that this process of ascension is your birthright, it is a reclaiming of that which belongs to you by natural law. You were born to be light and free, and not to suffer. We are here to help you to reclaim that which is already yours - a light, clear energy and a happy, joyful life.

Shall we begin?

WHO IS METATRON?

We would like to introduce ourselves to you.

Many of you know of us as Archangel Metatron and this is correct. We walked the Earth as the prophet Enoch many lifetimes ago. We also are known as the Lord Metatron and this is another of one of our many names.

The name you call us matters not. What does matter is that we are a multidimensional being of the highest light. We are more of a consciousness than a being. We radiate the love from Source, and we are here to assist humans with ascension and many other endeavors including their lightwork.

We are here to spread the message that humans no longer need to suffer and that all can live in joy.

We are multidimensional, as you would say, because we can travel to any dimension or reality, as well as to the past and to the future. There is nowhere in the universe where we cannot safely and competently go. Many beings, even light beings, are stationed in a certain dimension or area of the universe, so our ability to transcend space and time gives us a huge amount of flexibility. We can go everywhere, at once if we desire, and still be always and eternally one with Source energy. This is our gift. So we can assist each of you all at the same time and wherever it is required.

We can do no harm, and we are formed of pure light. We work with the angelic messengers of light, and we share a vision for the Earth, of wholeness, love and radiant light. You will surely feel the level of our light as you read this publication. This is no accident.

At this moment on the planet, many are heeding our call. We call those who will gladly stand beside us to usher in this new age and to welcome humans into the loving embrace of the ascended light. There is no need to suffer any longer. There is no longer a need for violence, poverty and struggle. Suffering breeds more suffering, and just the same, and even more, joy breeds more joy.

The more who hear our call and step into their power, the more the planet becomes a more beautiful and joyful place for all.

This is our work. This can be your work, too, if you so agree. If you are reading this book, then you are indeed called to work with METATRON to bring in more and more light.

This is joyful work and has the highest job satisfaction. We look forward to your reply (we can hear when you agree, even if it is in your thoughts).

For now, let us continue with our journey together.

Your Strategy for Personal Ascension

We have heard your questions, saying "Metatron, I do want to change and lighten my energies, but I know not how." Do not fear, friend, for you are never alone. We are your ever-present companion, and we are here to assist you with this process and anything else you wish.

There are several steps to a personal ascension process (according to Metatron) and they are all equally important. So you could say that each of them is on your to-do list at once and not one has any more importance than the other.

For the purposes of clarity, we will choose an order for our discussion.

Releasing the Past

We will first discuss releasing the past and transforming any negative effect it has had on you. Dear friend, you cannot rise above how you feel now if you are not willing and ready to examine how past events have affected you and how they could be draining your energy even to this day. This is a crucial step and is overlooked by many. We know it takes great bravery to confront what has impacted you so deeply, and yet we will not cease to ask you to do this - for EVERY event and relationship that has created a negative impact for you. No stone can be left unturned. This will take time and that is perfectly fine. The important thing is to begin. Of course, we are there to help you each step of the way.

As you release the past, you will find that your heart naturally begins to open up, and you will feel more love, for yourself and for all. This is a natural progression and delightful to experience.

Energy Upgrades

We are able, if you agree, to bring you changes in frequency we refer to as energy upgrades. From our elevated frequency of light, we are able to calibrate certain systemic changes in your energy fields just by exposing you to increasing levels of light. We do not mean light like that which comes from your sun. We refer to the LIGHT - as in the oneness and energy frequency which fuels the universe. We refer to light as the highest vibration of energy that exists in any reality or dimension. It is TRUTH and it transforms all it touches. We are experts at making sure that you receive the exact transmission of light which is required to elevate your energetic frequency and allow you to release the past even more easily. Indeed, when you allow our energy upgrades, many old "issues" dissolve without any effort whatsoever.

Awareness

We ask that, on an ongoing basis, you become aware of your own energy state. As you are navigating your life, you will have many choices presented to you. Some will deviate you from your path, even if slightly, and some will contribute to your personal growth and evolution (what we call your "highest good"). We ask that you work with us to develop an understanding and a sense of when your energy field is balanced and aligned, and also a sense of and a trust in the imbalanced or uncomfortable feeling that arises when something is out of alignment for you and will not contribute to your highest good. We will give you many techniques and strategies for making this assessment, and we are always happy to provide direct assistance as well.

However, while we are a being of the LIGHT, so are you. You may not feel this way at the moment but this is truth. Thus, we are now forming a partnership to work together which requires effort from you. We, as Metatron, cannot do everything for you because this would not lead to your optimal growth and development. That is why we will teach you techniques to carry out on your own.

As your awareness grows, we ask that you continue to be aware of the spiritual lessons we will bring to you and of your newfound observations about everything. It can be useful to begin an inspired journal for this purpose.

CHAPTER 2
Releasing the Past

W**E WILL FIRST** start with an explanation of why it is so important to release your past. You cannot have a light, bright future if you are still holding onto painful memories from the past. They hang on you like chains, the ever-present albatross weighing you down and dragging you back into unpleasant memories, feelings and thoughts. Indeed, even if you are not aware that you have this old energy weighing you down, unless you have purposefully reviewed and released it, we assure you that you do.

Even under the surface, and without your conscious awareness, energy from the past - painful memories or experiences - can seriously impact and undermine your future. We strongly advise you to follow our guidance and release yourselves from the ongoing impact of past events.

Here are some examples of past events which may have a negative effect on your future:

- Childhood trauma or abuse

- Bullying or social problems at school or within the family

- Other family issues

- Relationship difficulties, friendship and romantic

- Loss of a loved one

- Illness of yourself or of a loved one

- Other hardships that can be particularly difficult for those who are sensitive

We do not wish to convey the message that we do not sympathize with your pain, for we do, more than you know. If you are reading this book, then we were indeed with you throughout your life and even before. We were silently by your side, supporting you and loving you through each of your hardships. It is true that we have held a long connection, and we have never left your side. You may not believe this truth at the present moment, and yet, as you begin to trust us more and become more familiar with our energy, you will begin to believe more and more that we have always been with you.

We do not wish to make light of what you have been through. We appreciate the severity and the hurt it has caused you. We would like to help you to see your way to the other side of the pain.

Releasing the Past Exercise

Ages 0-10

We would like to start by asking you to complete a journal. We would like to remind you that you are free to seek the help of a professional human (healer, counselor or therapist) at any point to help you with any of this. For any extreme abuse or trauma, we strongly recommend that you do seek professional help from a trained and qualified human. You can still follow this process, but with their support and additional guidance.

Otherwise, we will proceed together.

In this journal, please outline the following ages:

0-1:

2-4:

5-7:

8-10:

Beside each age, we would like for you to make a brief list of the **most** significant painful experiences that happened during that time period. Try not to get caught up in the emotion of any of the occurrences, but just make the list for now.

There is a worksheet for you to use in this book. You also can download it here–

www.kristintaylorintuitive.com/ascensionbook
(Worksheet 1, password: lightwork)

On the worksheet, there is a space for "Persons Involved," which you will fill in later.

After you have compiled your list, we will help you transform the emotion of the occurrences, should you so desire (please let us know silently or aloud whether you agree to this).

Meditation

If you agree, please sit silently, imagining our presence and visualizing being bathed in very bright white light. Imagine your list also being bathed in this white light. Please be sure that you will have no distractions or interruptions. You can do a guided meditation if it is easier for you.

Please complete this with us (around 10 minutes) daily for one week. Please do try to be regular with this practice for it is the easier way we know for humans to release old energy, yet it requires consistency.

You will find a guided meditation for this exercise here–

www.kristintaylorintuitive.com/ascensionbook
(Meditation 1, password: lightwork)

WORKSHEET 1		
Releasing the Past Journal Page - Ages 0-10		
Age	Event	Persons Involved
0-1		
2-4		
5-7		
8-10		

Once 7 days have passed, please review your list again. If there is anything that is no longer painful, please cross it off. If there is something that still holds a painful memory or brings feelings of discomfort, please circle it.

Your next week will be focused around those circled events which are still painful to remember. Once again we ask that you meditate daily.

On the first day's meditation of the second week, please work with us on the first circled event on your list. Sit quietly and invoke us (either on your own or with a guided meditation) and again make sure that you will have no interruptions while we are working together. This is very important.

Bring that first painful event to mind and see the whole thing (everyone involved, the place and yourself) bathed in white light. If any feelings arise, allow them to come up and be sure to fully feel all of them. If you need to cry, allow yourself to cry. Whatever feeling you are feeling is perfectly acceptable in that moment. Continue to focus on the white light surrounding and infusing the situation. You can even imagine us - the Archangel Metatron - directly assisting with the situation and comforting you. Follow this process through until you feel you have some relief - perhaps less pain or perhaps a feeling of comfort.

Repeat the procedure the following day until

you no longer feel activated by the memory, as in you no longer have painful memories associated with it.

Work down your list day by day until you feel relief from all of the events. Do not be overwhelmed. You are not alone.

Once you have worked through your lifeline until the age of 10, please congratulate yourself. Know that we are also congratulating you. Is there a small treat you could allow yourself in recognition of this achievement?

Ages 11-21

The next step, when you feel ready, is to write down in your journal any significant events which occurred from ages 11-21 in the same manner as above.

Follow the same procedure, knowing that if ever things feel too much, you can turn to a professional for guidance and support at a human level.

You can use Worksheet 2 in this book to create your list, and you can use the same guided meditation as before, Both can be found here–

www.kristintaylorintuitive.com/ascensionbook
(Worksheet 2 & Meditation 1, password: lightwork)

WORKSHEET 2
Releasing the Past Journal Page - Ages 11-21

Age	Event	Persons Involved
11-13		
14-16		
17-19		
20-21		

Once you have completed those ages, please do give yourself a reward! You deserve it.

Ages 22 Onwards

Now list any significant events from age 22 until your present age. Please only list the most significant which caused you the most pain and which still cause extreme discomfort when you think of them.

Repeat the process once again, working with us to bring light and healing to each instance where you feel pain and hurt from your past.

You can use Worksheet 3 for this list, and you can listen to the same guided meditation as before. Both can be downloaded here–

www.kristintaylorintuitive.com/ascensionbook
(Worksheet 3 & Meditation 1, password: lightwork)

WORKSHEET 3
Releasing the Past Journal Page - Ages 22-Present

Age	Event	Persons Involved

It is worth noting that we - the Archangel Metatron - will be bringing you insights and observations along the way. We will be highlighting to you when you have learned important soul lessons from your past pain and reminding you that you no longer need to learn in this manner. We also will be reminding you of deeper spiritual lessons when appropriate.

Once again, we do not mean to oversimplify what you have been through nor do we wish to propose an oversimplified solution. Please remember that what may sound simple, is actually a solution that works with extremely high otherworldly technology provided by us. Things are not always as they seem.

FORGIVENESS EXERCISE

If you feel ready, the next step would be to take your initial lists of painful memories and write next to them the names of all of the humans who were involved and who hurt you. You can use the column on your worksheet entitled "Persons Involved" for this purpose. We expect that there will be many names of family members as this is the case with all of the sensitive lightworkers and healers, and with many others as well.

Do not be alarmed if, even after all of your efforts and work with us, there is still some pain when you complete this list. This is normal and expected.

As an example, your list will now look like this for each age range:

0-1:

[significant painful event] [persons involved]

[significant painful event] [persons involved]

2-4:

[significant painful event] [persons involved]

[significant painful event] [persons involved]

You can continue with this process, following the format on Worksheets 1-3.

An actual page could look something like this:

5-7:

Felt lack of love from mother: mother

8-10:

Bullying at school: Tommy, James and Arthur

We hope you are getting the idea of this.

Meditation

For those who feel ready to proceed, sit down to do your daily meditation with us. Bring to mind the persons involved in the first, earliest painful event. Hopefully, by now, the event will no longer feel so painful anymore, and we believe this to be the case. With these persons in mind, please allow us to help you. Once again, imagine the very bright white light and our assistance (visualize our form as an archangel made of white light) coming to you and to the persons involved. If, and only if you feel ready, say to these persons from the first event, one by one: "I forgive you [name]. Be free. I release you to the light." Then visualize this person floating away from you as you set their energy free with your forgiveness.

You will find a guided meditation for this exercise here–

www.kristintaylorintuitive.com/ascensionbook
(Meditation 2, password: lightwork).

If you feel that this process of forgiveness is incomplete for you (in that you still feel painful or negative emotions towards the persons involved) then feel free to repeat this meditation, perhaps the next day.

If you continue to repeat the process but still feel unable to release the person or persons, then make a note of this and continue to the next event and the next persons. You will be able to return to any unfinished persons when you have completed your list, and we will be helping you to release along the way. So it may be easier to release them at a later time.

If you feel ready, work through your entire list of persons involved. Some will take more time and focused attention than others. You will start to have a sense of lessons learned through the process, for yourself as well as for the other person or persons. You will start to see the experiences as contributing to who you are today and, in time, you will see the most difficult interactions as the most lesson-filled and important for you.

Do not feel you have to rush these insights because they will happen naturally over time. In our work together, it is best to be open and ready for the next step, as much as you are able. Wisdom from us is easiest obtained when you are simply allowing and not trying too hard to receive it.

Length of the Process & Benefits

We expect that this overall process will take you some time. If you are very motivated, it could take you a few months, up to six months. If you are taking your time with it (which is perfectly fine as well), then it could take upwards of one year or more. We suggest that you do dedicate yourself to this procedure as much as you can. Your rewards are infinitely worth it, and you will begin to see this as you go along.

We do in fact require this same procedure in whatever form (and additional steps to be explained at future dates) of all of our students. This is the step that many human spiritual "teachers" have not adequately undertaken, and this is the reason why their work is not consistently originating from the highest levels and light of existence.

Even if you do not seek to be a spiritual teacher or spread light in this capacity, this procedure will lead to astonishingly increased levels of happiness, joy, contentment, peace, flow, presence, and awareness. Not to mention that it increases your ability to work with the universe, in that you will be able to create your reality by what is called "manifesting" (along with some further instruction which we will provide at a future date). Without diligently undertaking this procedure to release your past, you will not be able to manifest or create any reality of your choosing, for it is your past pain that would be creating everything for you by default.

We do not wish this scenario on anyone, least of all on you, dear friend. So, heed our word and please do try to carry out the procedure outlined here for your own self-healing and liberation.

As you continue to release your past, a beautiful side effect is that your heart will open up, and you will begin to feel a profound love for all of humanity. You will really start to LOVE others from a deep place inside of you. This is perfectly natural and expected.

We advise you to embrace this change as it occurs. We know we are asking you to accept many changes, and for some of you, in a short space of human time. Yet, we ask that you continue to flow with this energy of kindness and love towards others.

You also will develop a stronger sense of compassion for others and for their journeys. There are those of you who have felt "too much" all of your lives, and we can hear you asking, "How will I cope with feeling even more?" We do hear you, and please, rest assured, that as you increase your sense of loving kindness and caring for the world, you are concurrently learning to release any sense of attachment to anyone else's journey. You are truly starting to recognize that everyone is safe and in the perfect place, wherever they are on their path, even if it is different to yours.

This simultaneous understanding (of love for humankind and of releasing attachment) opens you up to the ONENESS in a most amazing way. You begin to really FEEL with all parts of you that everything is perfect, even if it is aligned in its misalignment. You see that others, even if they are on a path that you feel is against their highest good, are learning valuable lessons, and they will learn and grow from those experiences. You start to trust the wisdom and guidance of each soul, even if it looks contrary to you.

This is an important step and one to be acknowledged. For in this realization, you unlock the secrets of the universe and to a happy life. You begin to be able to be happy on the journey as well as at the destination, because everything is imperfectly perfect.

This does not mean that we do not advise following guidance, both your own and ours, should you so choose. You are on a different path than the masses. You have been called here, and you have been asked to work with Metatron.

We mean that you will develop an understanding and compassion for the whole, and for everyone being on a different journey and path, individual to his or her own soul's calling. You will start to see the beauty in what was previously seen as ugly and the refined even in the rough.

We do not wish to rush these realizations, and all will be understood in its own timing. We simply wish to point out this delightful wisdom that is waiting for you.

We will now explain the next step of your journey with us. We hope you are enjoying it as much as we are!

CHAPTER 3
Opening to Energy Upgrades

WE ARE ABLE to help you more than you know. We are a multidimensional consciousness or being of light (it matters not how you think of us) and so we are able to assist on many levels and layers of your being without any harm or disruption to your system.

All you have to do is connect to our frequency and agree to our energy upgrades or vibrational lifts - again, the name you give them does not really matter.

We work with technologies your human race is yet to understand and may not understand for quite some time. It matters not. What does matter is that this technology is available to you now, should you wish to accept it.

You may or may not be aware of it, but there are many parts of you, and they are not all on the Earth plane. Some of them exist in other places and in other times. You are truly a multidimensional being. To say that you are purely a human living an earthly life would be ridiculously inaccurate.

Accordingly, energy imbalances can exist in many different places and even time periods. If you are seeking healing only in this Earthly dimension, you might be looking in the wrong place.

We suggest that you do not look at all, and instead trust us to help you to resolve any multidimensional energy imbalances. We are most pleased to assist you in this (and in every capacity).

All we ask of you is to trust us (as much as you can, for this will grow) and to spend regular time connecting to us. We prefer to see you in a daily meditation with us, but we are also able to help you at other times, particularly when you are asleep.

Remember that we are unable to do any harm and any adjustments we make to your energy would be always for your truest happiness and highest good.

MEDITATION

You can meditate with us on your own or you are free to follow a guided meditation. Please take care to choose a meditation carefully for not all who say they are working with us are actually channeling our frequency.

A guided meditation that will bring you the energy upgrade most beneficial to you at the time can be found here–

www.kristintaylorintuitive.com/ascensionbook
(Meditation 3, password: lightwork).

If you choose to connect with us on your own, please follow these instructions.

Let us begin by sitting quietly together. Please do ensure that you will not be interrupted or distracted. It can help to align our energies if you think of us helping you. Please imagine a beautiful, large being of light - in the form of an angel if it assists you. We are made of pure light, and this is our form.

Please sit with your back straight if possible as we will be making adjustments to your spine. We would prefer for you to be awake and not asleep if possible. Perhaps it would thus serve you best to sit upright in a chair or on the floor.

Imagine next that white light - of the brightest

variety - is coming through your body. It doesn't matter where you imagine it coming from. It could be coming from the Earth or from above your head, for example.

Allow this beautiful, comforting, loving light to integrate with every part of you.

Take deep breaths and allow the light to merge with you more, as you become more comfortable and trust our presence even more.

Remember to take very deep, slow breaths, for we connect with you most deeply through your breath.

Try to continue to relax and let go even more, if you can. Try to really surrender to this beautiful, loving light.

The more you relax and allow our energy to be with you, the more benefit you will receive. We understand if you are scared or hesitant at first, but this should subside with time.

We suggest that you sit with us for energy upgrades at least once per week if not more often. You can sit with us daily if you wish.

You are always welcome to work with us and to benefit from our energy.

CHAPTER 4
Becoming Aware of Your Own Energetic Alignment

I T IS IMPORTANT to become aware of your own energy and how it is aligned at any given time. Building this awareness takes consistent attention.

You can think of it as becoming one with YOU - with all that you are. So many of you live your daily lives out of touch with your senses and feelings, unaware of your emotional states and not realizing when certain events or situations induce lower energy feelings.

To work at an advanced level with us, we require that you develop an awareness of your own energy and of your own emotional state. There is no shortcut to this.

We further ask you to strongly consider changing any situations or relationships which continue to cause you great levels of stress.

It is true that unresolved energies from your past can negatively influence your future, and this is something to bear in mind. You will likely have a feeling if this is the case, as you will not be quite ready to end the situation or relationship.

We are speaking of those situations which have clearly come to an end and, yet, you insist on staying anyway. This practice does not benefit anyone, least of all you, because it creates stagnation.

We will discuss this in further detail in this chapter.

Noticing Your Feelings

At this stage of our work together, we have another request for you. That is to begin to pay attention to your energy state, to how you are feeling at any given moment and what course of action or decision feels right to you.

We refer this as being in your **highest good** or truest happiness. It describes your highest expression of yourself as a radiant and joyful being on this planet, in this incarnation and in this body. It is how you feel, as you would say, the most like yourself and the happiest version of this. It's that feeling of really being in the right place at the right time.

We assert that you can feel this way all of the time if you just follow guidance (your own and ours) and pay attention. This allows you to merge with the universal flow of life - the Divine energy of ONE, the Divine flow. There are many names to this feeling but we assert that it simply feels "right." It is the feeling of not wanting to be anywhere else, doing anything else or with anyone else. Exactly where you are feels wonderful, and you feel happy, aligned and free.

This state is easier reached when you have completed or are regularly undertaking the other two steps (releasing the past and allowing energy upgrades from us), yet this happy state of mind also is cultivated. It is practiced and developed. It is not by accident nor is it haphazard.

If you wish to become a student of Archangel Metatron, let us explain this process to you. Of course, this is always your choice and you are free to discontinue our recommended practices at any time. We deeply bow to your sovereignty and infinitely respect your free will. Only you can make the choices that you feel are best for you.

Exercise

We wish you to begin by simply bringing an awareness into your everyday life of your feelings at every moment in time or as often as you can remember to observe them. Pay particular attention to changes in feelings, for example, from happy to sad or angry to excited. Especially watch for a feeling that something isn't quite right. You may feel this in your gut ("gut feeling") or it may be elsewhere in or throughout your body. It matters not.

What matters is that you start to observe your feelings and to honor them. We are not saying that you should renounce all of your commitments to others, but please start to be aware and accept all of your feelings.

You may wish to write them down in your journal. You could write something like the following:

[date] [time] [feeling] [external situation if any]

You can use your own journal or Worksheet 4 found this book. It can be downloaded here–

www.kristintaylorintuitive.com/ascensionbook
(Worksheet 4, password: lightwork).

WORKSHEET 4
Becoming Aware of Your Feelings

Date	Time	Feeling	External Situation (if any)

You might then review your journal at the end of the week to see if you always have the same feeling in certain situations. For example, perhaps you always feel anxious or sad at work. That could be a signal that you would benefit from some relaxation techniques in relation to work, some help from us (please ask if so) or perhaps you could benefit from opening to a new job or career.

We have said it before and we will say it again and again until you have all heard us: **YOU ARE NOT HERE ON EARTH TO SUFFER!** Suffering is unnecessary. If you are feeling consistently upset or anxious about something, you can work on this energy to change it or it may call for finding a new situation, work or relationship. **Perpetual suffering helps no one!** It is completely useless.

Yet so many of you are so unaware of your feelings that you miss the signs that clearly and without a doubt indicate that it is time to move on from that situation, work or relationship. Many of you deny that something no longer resonates with you. In this way, you can become delayed (or "stuck" as many of you like to say) on your true path - which is moving along with the current and the flow of life.

We do not wish for you to become obsessed with this tracking of your feelings. That is not the point. The point is to help you to identify how you are feeling when you are unaware and notice how these feelings feel in your body, especially when something feels "right" or aligned. The point also is to identify any situations or relationships which perpetually lower your energy.

Letting Go & Welcoming the New

As you change and grow, particularly if you are accelerating your spiritual path (for all are on the spiritual path whether they know it or not), you will surely "outgrow" certain situations and relationships. This is fact. But how do you handle it next? Do you gracefully let them go and embrace the new, lighter energies being brought to you by the Divine flow? Or do you drag your feet, kicking and screaming, refusing to let go of the old and, thus, refusing to make way for the brighter, happier new?

You may not believe us but we do assert (and it is fact) that everything is improving all the time. Thus the workplace you loved 10 years ago may no longer be a vibrational match to your new energy.

Can we stop seeing this kind of change as a punishment and start to see it as a promotion? The universe has just promoted you to a lighter and brighter situation. Isn't that a cause for celebration rather than dwelling on whatever has had to be released in order to make way for the new?

41

We believe and know that it is cause for celebration. How you see this (letting go and accepting the new) is all a matter of how much you trust the goodness of the universe. If you truly believe and trust that everything is working out for your highest good and truest happiness and that your life is always getting better and better, then letting go of the old creates a kind of excitement and a beautiful anticipation of what is to come next.

If you do not feel this level of trust yet, do not worry. The more time we spend together (in the course of the exercises laid out in this book), the more you will naturally begin to trust the universe and the more your energy will change to gracefully let go of the old, elegantly and effortlessly accepting the beautiful new.

MAKING DECISIONS FOR YOUR HIGHEST GOOD

We wish to explain to you the impact your decision-making has on your energy state and level of happiness.

We have previously asked you to become aware of what feels right to you and to track your feelings at any given time.

We hope that you will get a sense from this exercise of the feeling of when things feel "right." This is a feeling of alignment.

We wish for you to try to memorize how this feeling - the feeling of alignment - feels in your body. We wish for you to practice this feeling so much that you notice right away if a situation or relationship feels out of alignment to you in any way.

Now we do not mean to suggest that you leave your job or your romantic partner if you have a bad day. We are talking about those situations which **repeatedly** feel wrong to you - out of alignment - and as if you are in the wrong place at the wrong time. There is a sense of deep uneasiness about the situation or relationship and, if you were honest with yourself, deep down you know that this situation is not for you. For whatever reason, usually fear, you have chosen to not leave the situation, and this creates more and more stagnant energy in your energy field.

Exercise

We ask that you now undertake a review of your life to see if there are any situations which match this description. We are not asking for hasty action here such as leaving your job. You are still on the Earth plane and must respect the natural laws, meaning it is sensible to take your time with any decisions, especially if they are important. Just because you are working with an archangel of light does not mean that we can magically solve everything for you. In short, this is not possible because of other factors at play, including that you would not learn your lessons if we did this.

So we are asking you to make an investigation of any situations or relationships which are not **adding to your happiness** at least most of the time. We ask that once you determine, and please take your time with this decision, that these situations are not serving your highest and best good, to work to **transition** out of these situations. We are of course here to help you every step of the way.

We do advise that you make a **firm decision** of what you would like to do. We cannot assist near as much if you keep changing your mind ("I'm leaving," then "I'm staying," then "I'm leaving," etc.). A clear and fully committed decision receives the most assistance from the universe, in every case.

Meditation - How to Align Your Energy

When you have become accustomed to feeling your feelings and to your energy state at any given time, the next step is to purposefully enter into a state of "alignment." We are happy to assist you with this each and every time you do it.

To induce a state of alignment, complete these steps in order:

1. Sit quietly with your feet on the floor. You must then pay attention to your feet. Notice how they touch the floor. Although it is easier to be sitting in a chair, if you are sitting on the floor, notice how part of your body is touching the floor.

2. With your awareness on your feet, imagine that you have roots similar to a tree extending deep down into the core of the Earth. Visualize these roots extending down several times.

3. Now bring your awareness to your body. Imagine that you have a beam of white light coming from the universe above your head and then down into your head, through your body, down to your root chakra at the base of the spine, and into the Earth. Make sure you are breathing deeply throughout this process. Keep imagining this beam of very bright white light until it feels very real to you. This white light should run directly through your spine.

4. Now imagine the white beam of light extending to the width of your body, still connecting you to the universe above and to the Earth below.

5. Imagine that it extends further than your

body until it is all around you, enveloping you in brilliant, beautiful light.

6. Breathe deeply and feel how aligned your energy is at this moment.

We wish for you to complete this brief exercise in the morning before starting your day and at any time throughout the day when you feel you have gone out of alignment. When you get more practiced at it, you also can do it standing up, if you like.

As an optional step, you can add that, as you are breathing, at the very end, you imagine feeling empowered and that you have received all of the resources you need for your day, as well as happiness and joy, right within your column of light. You can breathe them in and feel them change your energy field.

You could also imagine that we are there with you, and, if you like, that we are merging with your energy field, giving you the beautiful and magnificent energy and loving presence of the Archangel Metatron.

You will find a guided meditation for this exercise here–

www.kristintaylorintuitive.com/ascensionbook
(Meditation 4, password: lightwork).

We wish you a wonderful day, each and every day!

QUICK DAILY MEDITATION - CLEANSING YOUR ENERGY

We also suggest a practice for the end of your day.

There are a number of energies out in the world and not all of them are beneficial for you to keep in your energy field. You are a sensitive person, and it is vitally important for you to keep your energy field clean. By saying "clean," we mean free of lower energies, residues and, as much as possible, negative emotions.

We know that many of you already know energy cleansing procedures, but may we ask, how many of you actually do them on a regular basis? Have you done them enough to know that they actually work and make a huge difference to how you feel? We would say you have not and that you do not know (yet).

If you are willing to try, we are always more than willing to teach you.

The practice is simple. At the end of your day and before you go to bed, follow these steps:

1. Call on us, the Archangel Metatron to assist

you with this process (and with anything else you require at the time).

2. Imagine that you are creating a ball of light between your hands. You can rub your hands together and really visualize that this ball of light grows the more you focus on it. Really get a sense of palpable energy growing between your hands.

3. Take your hands and place them above your head. Imagine that this ball of light immediately extends down into your entire body and energy field, enveloping you in a column or beam of white light. Know that this beam of light is made of the highest energy in the universe - brilliant white light.

4. Imagine that you are taking a virtual bath in the energy of this beautiful column and allow it to penetrate every part of your being - both at the physical and spiritual levels.

5. When you are ready, you can let go of the visualization and go to bed.

By doing this exercise every night, you are actually helping to boost your alignment and help yourself to (1) become aligned more of the time with less effort; and (2) bring yourself into more attunement with our energy, which helps to keep you aligned as well.

The whole process should take no longer than a few minutes, but consistency is important. Try this for one week without judgment, then see how you feel. You may wish to record the results of your experiments in your journal.

You will find a guided meditation for this exercise here–

www.kristintaylorintuitive.com/ascensionbook
(Meditation 5, password: lightwork).

CHAPTER 5
Conclusion & Further Work

W E ARE SO pleased with your efforts so far. We are hoping you also are proud of yourself and that you will celebrate your progress! You have taken steps which many humans are very afraid to take.

We would like to explain further steps we can take together, if you are willing and only when you feel ready.

We can more closely merge our energies in a process known as "channeling." Channeling is for increased well-being (due to the energies involved) and for guidance. It should only be done with a consciousness or being of the highest light. It is not a game, and it is not to be undertaken lightly.

The benefits are joyous, including a

much-increased sense of well-being, joy, happiness, and purpose. In the course of the process, you "borrow" our frequency in structured sessions in order to benefit from our elevated vibration. The effect is cumulative, meaning that as you relax and trust us more, you receive increasing benefit until you realize that your life has completely changed for the better.

Channeling is another topic which is not relevant to this book.

We encourage you to undertake further studies with us when you see fit. Please do be aware that not all teachers are qualified or appropriate for this kind of study. Great inner work has to be done as well as connection with the Divine in order to prepare a channel and even more has to be undertaken for a teacher. It takes dedication and commitment to regularly and accurately access the highest realms.

For now, we wish to bid you farewell. Or we should say, until we meet again. This book has come to an end, and thus so have our teachings at this stage in your journey. We wish you all the best on this adventure we are taking together. Please do remember that you can ask us any question - even in your mind - and we will find a way to answer it, even if it is through another situation in your life or another person. You are never alone. So please do begin to pay attention to us working in your life. It will increase more and more (in a beautiful way) the more you attune to our energy and the more you work with us.

With all of our love and greatest appreciation of you and all that you are,

ARCHANGEL METATRON

CHAPTER 6
Case Studies

ARCHANGEL METATRON ASKED me to teach a weekly advanced channeling class. It would be called Channeling Archangel Metatron, Advanced Class and would be a live, online class lasting 1.5 hours. I was asked to invite the students he selected, which were located across the globe.

In the group, every week, we have a theme that I channel from Metatron then the students practice channeled readings for each other. It is part mentoring (from me and from Metatron), part ascension support group and part channeling class. However we define it, the results have been magical. Every student in the small class has grown, changed and advanced remarkably. All of us, including me, look forward to the class every week, which I have taught no matter what else is going on in my life, as I was asked to do by Metatron. Below are some of the students' case studies and comments.

SCARLETT

Scarlett (not her real name) is a spiritual woman in her early 70s living in the USA. She has trained in Reiki and other healing modalities. When she came to our advanced Channeling Archangel Metatron class, she had several autoimmune disorders and very high blood pressure. She was in extreme pain.

She was deeply unhappy and felt quite hopeless. The doctors could do nothing for her but give her medication, which did not completely help. One of her medications, a steroid, made her gain 30 pounds and caused her to look very puffy. She could not travel for several years and deeply wished to visit her daughter in Europe. For a time, she was even unable to drive.

Nonetheless, Scarlett attended the classes and did the homework without expectation or attachment. She noticed she was feeling better, then during a period of two weeks in early 2018, she completely healed.

Her family was and continues to be shocked, especially those who do not believe in healing. They still expect her to be sick, and she keeps reminding them that she is now completely well.

She wasted no time to book her plane ticket to visit her daughter in Europe and had a wonderful visit with no issues.

Scarlett 100% attributes her healing to the channeling class. She is feeling better and better each day. In addition to the healing, she keeps getting happier and happier. She is light and joyful. Other parts of her life have blossomed as well, including her relationships and her newfound focus on painting.

Scarlett works with angelic energy on a daily basis, and she has found that it helps her with all kinds of things. She loves to say, "Metatron helps with everything."

As an example, one time she had to go to a family dinner with very difficult people. Always before, she had left these gatherings feeling drained. This time, she asked for help from Metatron in advance. She was absolutely amazed that the dinner went extremely well and no one acted badly, for the first time ever.

Scarlett has worked with angelic energy (via sessions with Kristin and meditation on her own) to look much younger. As a result, she looks 20-30 years younger than her contemporaries. She is often asked by her friends if she has had cosmetic surgery or some other medical intervention, but she has not. Angelic energy has made her feel and look more radiant, dynamic and younger. It has made her glow from within.

Relying on angels has become an indispensable part of Scarlett's everyday life. They have helped her to feel an indescribable calm, peace and confidence about her future. They have completely changed her life for the better.

Scarlett worked through the processes in this book and felt a beautiful sense of clarity and peace. She felt Metatron's energy running through her body, and this deepened her connection with him. Since then, she has had even more direct guidance from him, and this has upgraded her energy and helped her to make an important decision for the next chapter of her life.

Yolanda

I feel so grateful and blessed to have found Kristin a few years ago. I was living in physical pain and generally unhappy. Life had been difficult, and I was at the end of my emotional tether.

Kristin was my last resort as the medical profession seemed unable to help me. I came to Kristin for healing and had no knowledge or awareness of Archangel Metatron. I had no conscious connection to angels before this.

After some time as a client of Kristin's, I became a student, too. I started doing daily work with Metatron, first through guided meditations. Through Kristin's classes, I later learned to work with Metatron on my own, too. I prefer working with him myself now because I am able to tailor my meditations to what he and I feel is important for me at the time.

Since becoming one of Kristin's channeling students and working with Metatronic energy I have become happier and happier. I am absolutely elated to have this direct connection to the divine. My life has completely transformed. I am pain-free now. I'm much less anxious and fearful. I'm very happy nearly all the time. If I have a wobble and start feeling low, I now have the skills and connection to quickly get back on track.

Magical things have happened since I began working with Archangel Metatron. My relationships have become more loving. Most importantly, my relationship with myself has improved a hundredfold! I am so much more positive about life.

Life feels so much easier whereas it used to be such a struggle. There's so much more joy and beauty in my life on a daily basis.

In this book, Archangel Metatron recommends facing your fears. Coming from a challenging background, I had many fears that were difficult to face. With Kristin's and Archangel Metatron's help, I confronted even my deepest fears and reclaimed my life as a result. My advice to you is that facing your fears takes a lot of courage, but the results are so worth it.

Archangel Metatron's energy is extremely transformative, especially when you engage with it on a daily basis. I can promise that if you decide to work with him, you will be glad that you did. His energy feels amazing - so light and loving. It's also incredibly amazing to have access to guidance and love from such a beautiful being!

He's like a best friend who only ever has your best interests at heart. He's so supportive, and you never ever feel judged.

I never expected or saw this coming. And yet working with Metatron has been miraculous for me. If I can completely transform my life, you can, too!

- Yolanda Earl, Business Owner, UK

SALVO

I met Kristin about two years ago when I posted something about crystal healing on Facebook. She introduced me to the energy of Metatron and the incredible changes life could take.

As an ex-Catholic, I knew about angels and archangels but for me, to contact Metatron, the archangel closest to God, was not a thing to take so lightly. So, I admit that at the beginning I was a bit skeptical. Slowly Kristin showed me how safe and reliable Metatronic energy is.

Archangel Metatron is never forceful, judgmental nor critical of our human experience. He makes me feel safe whenever his presence is close. Every day I feel this connection becoming stronger and stronger, and I like the idea I can trust Metatron to help me even with simple things. I am a crystal healer, and my crystal healing method has changed. The way I relate to people has changed, and my entire vision of the world has changed. Synchronicities regularly happen in my life, and Metatron inspires my work daily.

One of the things that really surprised me was the call to work with Metatron. In one of the channeling sessions Kristin did for me, Metatron confirmed that it was divinely aligned for me to work with him as I decided to do so in my previous life. That for me was a sign that I was and am on the right path.

Metatron made me understand that I needed to improve myself if I wanted positive changes in my life. So the big push for me is to be in the right frame of mind to help others as a healer. It's a simple process but it requires a self-caring and self-loving attitude.

I followed the steps in this book, I healed my past and sent love and light to the people who upset me. It's astonishing how things have improved - relationships with loved ones and co-workers that sometimes could be upsetting are now easily mended, asking for a smooth working day when things get tricky always helps, and even my cat is less fussy. Being with Metatron's energy also improves my mood when I'm down and helps me to find the positive sides of things.

Now I regularly take Kristin's advanced Metatron classes where our daily experiences with Metatron are shared and our energy lifted by the direct channeling by Kristin of his energy. These really give us all a boost for an amazing week.

For these reasons, I would like to thank you, Kristin and Metatron, for being a part of my life!

- Salvo Scalici, Crystal Healer, UK

ELAINE

I found Kristin several years ago. I was at a point in my life where I felt overwhelmed both personally and professionally, and I had long had a secret interest in alternative healing, and understanding how to work with my own intuition. But I thought people, especially my family, would laugh or think I was foolish. But my health was being affected and conventional medicine wasn't changing that. It was just damping it down for a time here and there.

I reached out to Kristin and we soon met. From the outset, her kind and gentle presence and her patience calmed and reassured me, and we began the process of releasing.

I worked with Kristin over several years before she introduced me to Archangel Metatron. But as soon as she did it was clear that this was where my path had been leading all along. The health issues drifted away and my sense of calm returned and grew.

I am in Kristin's advanced channeling class, and, in it, we continue to let go and release all that we need to in a safe and supportive environment. The group is purposefully small, but the energy is vast and beautiful. We laugh and joke, we build each other up and we listen, all in Archangel Metatron's company, with his guidance and in the warmth of his light.

It is a life-changing experience, and it is truly a gift. We are also given the tools and the confidence to work with Metatron on our own terms in our own time. And the tools to manage our own energy on a daily basis.

Probably the greatest part of this gift is knowing that Metatron is always with us, and is always there to help and guide us. We just have to ask. Knowing this and asking for help has helped me to manage difficult days, sticky relationships with colleagues, friends, and families and to learn that no matter how lonely I might feel from time to time, I never really am alone. None of us are.

Thank you. Kristin, for guiding us here and for sharing your experience and guidance with us!

- Elaine, Designer, Italy

Glossary of Terms

Alignment: The process whereby a human being aligns his or her energy with the Divine, causing a state of great peace and relaxation. There are techniques for achieving this beneficial state and regular practice is recommended.

Ascension: We refer to this as "personal ascension." This is the process whereby a human purposefully takes steps to lighten his or her energy, thereby creating a collective effect on the whole of the planet. The importance of this process cannot be overemphasized, for it is crucial for all who feel called to undertake the steps outlined in this book, for the benefit of the Earth and of all humans. This process is critically important, and we, the Archangel Metatron, are here to help every step of the way.

Divine: All that emanates from Source energy - God

- the ONENESS, all that is, there are many names and it matters not what you call it. We use this term to indicate the highest level of consciousness, also called the highest light.

Energy Upgrade: We, the Archangel Metatron, have offered to assist your personal growth and ascension by working with you to uplift and transform your energy field with the highest light. We use high-level spiritual technology to assist you to raise your vibration and to help you to release the past more easily. We do this while you meditate with us, and, upon request, also while you sleep.

Highest Good: This is you in your happiest state and truest expression of YOU, of who you came here to be, without the encumbrances of fear or unresolved energy from your past.

Light: We refer here to the HIGHEST DIVINE LIGHT which is the technology we use to complete our work. Light is intelligence, and it has technology and abilities beyond current human comprehension. We recommend that you begin to become proficient at working with us and with Light.

Lightworker: There is some confusion over what this term actually means. According to us, the Archangel Metatron, a "lightworker" is one who has the feeling in his or her heart of wanting to better the planet and is drawn to doing this by means of spiritual practices. We also speak of "wayshowers," which are a subset of lightworkers, who are working very closely with the Light to illuminate the way for other lightworkers and for the planet. We deeply and humbly bow to all who have heard this call, and we so very much appreciate working with you all, in whichever capacity and at any level.

Multidimensional: There are many, many dimensions and even universes in existence. To think that you, as Earthlings, are alone in the universe is simply not true. When we refer to more than one dimension, reality or timeline, than this current existence on Earth, we use the term "multidimensional" to denote the multiplicity. As a student of Metatron, we ask that you begin to become aware of the multidimensional nature of existence, for this understanding helps our work greatly.

Oneness: Also known as the Divine or Source, God, and many other names. We use this term to denote that all is ONE. This is a realization that will become more apparent after you have studied with us for some time.

Source: Also known as the Divine, God or the ONENESS. All is Source energy, and yet it is a useful practice to connect directly to Source. We, the Archangel Metatron, are part of Source energy, as are you, dear friend. Yet, it is possible to feel more or less aligned with Source at any given time. The longer you practice with us, the closer you will feel aligned with Source energy.

Spiritual Path: This term describes the journey you are undertaking with us at this moment, but also probably began before discovering our work together. It is the process of being called to work with the healing arts, doing spiritual practices, obtaining spiritual insights, and generally lightening your energy field. There are many ways to undertake the spiritual path, and working with Metatron is but one. We respect all methods, and yet some of you are directly called to work with us. You know who you are.

Wayshower: See Lightworker

About Kristin Taylor

KRISTIN TAYLOR IS a channel, intuitive healer, spiritual mentor, teacher, and artist dedicated to helping her students and clients reach their highest potential, deepen their spiritual connection and live high vibration lives.

A natural intuitive, Kristin was aware of her gifts from a young age. She began exploring energy work over fifteen years ago when she discovered Reiki healing. Her experience with Reiki inspired her to pursue further spiritual training, including other healing modalities, medical intuition, channeling, mediumship, and psychic development.

Kristin is an expert at spiritual channeling, which involves contacting high-level beings for support and guidance. She has been working with her main guide, Archangel Metatron, since 2006.

She teaches channeling so that others may connect to the angels' energy, love and wisdom.

She has personally experienced the impact that healing and spiritual work can bring to a person's life. Kristin has had several chronic health conditions healed, life situations dramatically improved and emotional issues resolved.

Kristin is dedicated to empowering lightworkers. She recently founded the Lightworkers Training Academy, an online school dedicated to training lightworkers in essential skills and advancing their spiritual development.

Her work has been the subject of media attention including Psychologies magazine and London's Evening Standard magazine.

Kristin is a qualified lawyer and worked for several years in corporate law in the City of London. She holds BA (in Studio Art), JD and LLM degrees. She speaks fluent French.

She is based in London, UK and works internationally. Kristin is originally from Colorado Springs, Colorado, USA. She also has lived in New Orleans, Perpignan and Paris.

Kristin creates spiritual art. Her paintings fulfill different energetic purposes, transforming and uplifting the energy around them.

About Kristin Taylor

In her spare time, Kristin enjoys salsa dancing, being outdoors, traveling, and gourmet cooking.

To receive weekly updates and special channeled messages from Kristin, subscribe on her website:

🌐 Website:
https://www.kristintaylorintuitive.com

𝐟 Facebook:
Kristin Taylor Intuitive, https://www.facebook.com/kristintaylorintuitive/

📷 Instagram: Kristin Taylor Intuitive
https://www.instagram.com/kristintaylorintuitive/

▶ YouTube: Kristin Taylor Intuitive
https://www.youtube.com/channel/c/KristinTaylorIntuitive

Notes

NOTES

NOTES

NOTES

_____

_____

_____

_____

_____

_____

_____

_____

_____

_____

_____

_____

_____

_____

_____

_____

_____

_____

_____

_____

NOTES

NOTES

NOTES

_____
_____
_____
_____
_____
_____
_____
_____
_____
_____
_____
_____
_____
_____
_____
_____
_____
_____
_____
_____
_____

NOTES

_____

_____

_____

_____

_____

_____

_____

_____

_____

_____

_____

_____

_____

_____

_____

_____

_____

_____

_____

_____

_____

NOTES

NOTES

_____

_____

_____

_____

_____

_____

_____

_____

_____

_____

_____

_____

_____

_____

_____

_____

_____

_____

_____

_____

NOTES

NOTES

NOTES

NOTES

_____

_____

_____

_____

_____

_____

_____

_____

_____

_____

_____

_____

_____

_____

_____

_____

_____

_____

_____

_____

Printed in the USA
CPSIA information can be obtained
at www.ICGtesting.com
LVHW090543100224
771202LV00016B/24

9 781632 272881